WORLD SOCCER LEGENDS

STARS
OF ALL TIME

Abbeville Press Publishers
New York · London

A portion of this book's proceeds are donated to the **Hugo Bustamante AYSO Playership Fund**, a national scholarship program to help ensure that no child misses the chance to play AYSO Soccer. Donations to the fund cover the cost of registration and a uniform for a child in need.

Text by Illugi Jökulsson
Design and layout: Árni Torfason

For the English-language edition
Editor: Will Lach
Production manager: Louise Kurtz
Layout: Ada Rodriguez
Copy editor: Sharon Lucas

PHOTOGRAPHY CREDITS

Getty Images: p. 8 (Allsport), 10 (Bob Thomas), 12 (Keystone), 14 (Keystone), 17 (Allsport Hulton/Archive), 18 (Central Press), 20 (David Cannon/Allsport), 24 (Popperfoto), 26 (Allsport UK), 28 (David Cannon/Allsport), 30 (Central Press/Hulton Archive), 33 (Phil Cole), 36 (David Cannon/Allsport), 39 (VI Images), 43 (Allsport), 44 (Phil Cole), 49 (Clive Mason), 55 (Hulton Archive), 60 (Bongarts)

Shutterstock: p. 2–3 (Marcos Mesa Sam Wordley), 22 (CP DC Press), 33 (Paolo Bona), 35 (Marcos Mesa Sam Wordley), 52 (Maldini: Paolo Bona), 54 (mooinblack), 55 (Maxisport), 56 (Müller: Mitch Gunn), 56 (Xavi: YiAN Kourt), 56 (Iniesta: katatonia82), 57 (Ververidis Vasilis), 62 (Gines Romero)

Wikimedia Commons: p. 50 (Batistuta: eftir http://www.anses.gob.ar/), 50 (Santamaria: eftir óþekktur), 50 (Zanetti: eftir Steindy), 51 (Varela: eftir óþekktur), 54 (Meazza: eftir óþekktan), 55 (Riva: eftir óþekktur), 55 (Rivera: eftir óþekktur), 55 (Zoff: eftir óþekktur), 58 (AGIF), 59 (Eto: Paolo Bona), 59 (Toure: CosminIftode)

Árni Torfason: p. 46, 61

First published in the United States of America in 2017 by Abbeville Press, 655 Third Avenue, New York, NY 10017

First Edition
10 9 8 7 6 5 4

ISBN 978-0-7892-1295-5

Library of Congress Cataloging-in-Publication Data available upon request

For bulk and premium sales and for text adoption procedures, write to Customer Service Manager, Abbeville Press, 655 Third Avenue, New York, NY 10017, or call 1-800-Artbook.

Visit Abbeville Press online at www.abbeville.com.

CONTENTS

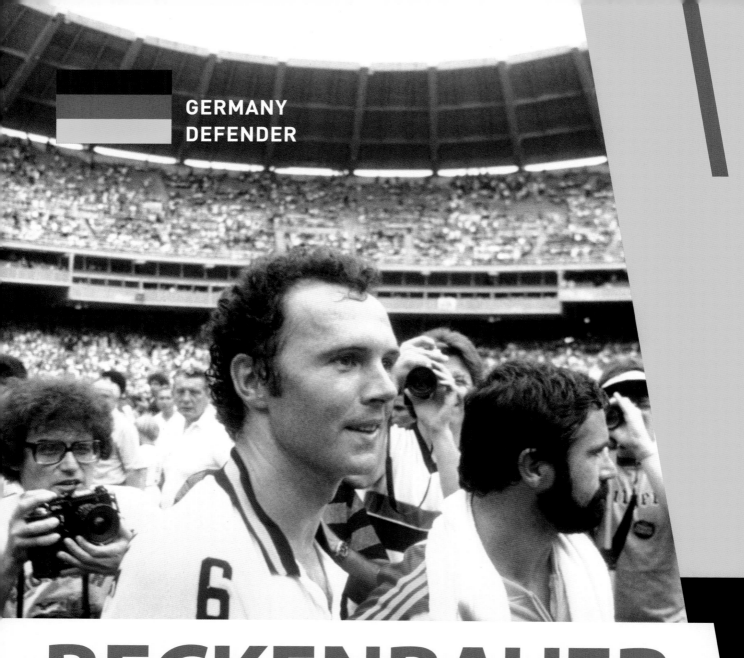

BECKENBAUER

Beckenbauer was such a towering figure with both Bayern München and the West German national team that even to this day, he is still called "The Emperor."

FRANZ BECKENBAUER
BORN: SEPTEMBER 11, 1945
WHERE: MÜNICH, GERMANY
HEIGHT: 5FT 11½IN

TEAMS:
BAYERN MÜNCHEN, GERMANY: 1964–1977
NEW YORK COSMOS, USA: 1977–1980, 1983
HAMBURG, GERMANY: 1980–1982

INTERNATIONAL GAMES: 1965–1977
TOTAL: 103
GOALS: 14

Beckenbauer was mostly positioned in defense, given his great strength and cunning. His signature move was to direct the ball from his team's goal, and set the ground for the offense. Beckenbauer often played as sweeper, a positon that is rare in contemporary soccer. The sweeper was often positioned behind the midfielders and was responsible for "sweeping up" the ball when it passed the defense, and immediately set the offense in motion, commonly via precision passes to wingers or forwards.

Beckenbauer was such an ingenious defense player and team leader that he is repeatedly noted as the greatest defender in history—without ever being rough or vicious. The most triumphant achievement of Beckenbauer's career was winning the World Cup for West Germany both as a player, and then 16 years later, as coach.

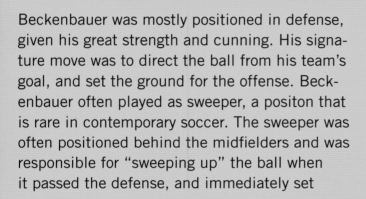

MAJOR HONORS
WORLD CUP CHAMPION: 1974
WORLD CUP RUNNER-UP: 1966
UEFA EUROPEAN CHAMPIONSHIP: 1972
GERMAN CHAMPION: FIVE TIMES
DFB-POKAL CHAMPION: FOUR TIMES
NORTH AMERICAN SOCCER LEAGUE
   CHAMPION: THRICE
EUROPEAN CUP: 1974, 1975, 1975
BALLON D'OR: 1972, 1976

MAJOR HONOR AS COACH
WORLD CUP CHAMPION: 1990
FRENCH CHAMPION: ONCE
GERMAN CHAMPION: ONCE
UEFA CUP: ONCE

BEST

GEORGE BEST
BORN: MAY 22, 1946
WHERE: BELFAST, NORTHERN IRELAND
DIED: NOVEMBER 25, 2005 (ONLY 59 YEARS OLD)

TEAM:
MANCHESTER UNITED, ENGLAND:
1963–1974

INTERNATIONAL GAMES:
1964–1977
TOTAL: 37
GOALS: 9

NORTHERN IRELAND
FORWARD

Best's biggest achievement was his involvement in bringing Manchester United the 1968 European Cup, the first English soccer team to win the title. And Best received the Ballon d'Or that same year. At that time, Best's fame was like that of a rock star, and he loved the spotlight and the accompanying parties. He was only 22 years old. However, the partying also contained his downfall, and Best's career quickly began to decline.

Despite the fact that modern soccer originates from England, and that the country has produced many of the world's greatest soccer players, their very best home player in England wasn't English; he was born in Northern Ireland. George Best entered the scene in the fall of 1963 as a player for Manchester United, at the tender age of 17, and he is one of the most admired players to ever represent that famous team. At his best, Best truly lived up to his name—he was an amazingly skillful and cunning left winger, and an eager goal scorer. During a time when players in England were mainly known for their strength, bulk, and even roughness, Best was a sight for sore eyes with his spirited energy and skill.

Some claimed that a Brazilian team would be a better match for his style. Unfortunately, his life outside soccer was beset with difficulties, which eventually led to the end of his career with Manchester United. Best struggled with severe alcoholism. After he left Manchester United, Best drifted between various lower-level teams for several years as his health continued to deteriorate. He continuously got himself into trouble, ignored his health, and then died a tragically untimely death. England, however, will always remember him as the joyous youngster who dazzled the audience with his wizardly skills.

MAJOR HONORS
PREMIER LEAGUE CHAMPION: 1965, 1967
EUROPEAN CUP: 1968
BALLON D'OR: 1968

JOHAN CRUYFF

BORN: APRIL 15, 1947
WHERE: AMSTERDAM, THE NETHERLANDS
DIED: MARCH 25, 2016
HEIGHT: 5FT 11IN

TEAMS:
AJAX, NETHERLANDS: 1964–1973, 1981–1983
BARCELONA, SPAIN: 1973–1979

INTERNATIONAL GAMES: 48
GOALS: 33

Cruyff was raised just a stone's throw away from Ajax's stadium, and grew up immersed in soccer. He counts among both the most intelligent and most agile players in soccer history. Cruyff was the originator and main symbol of the great soccer that characterized the Netherlands' style from around 1970. This style of play was called "Total Soccer" and involved the team's players working as one, both in offense and defense, and rotating positions depending on the requirements of the game. Cruyff mainly played forward, and scored beautiful goals of every kind. Undoubtedly, he figures on the list of top-five soccer players in the world, and following his illustrious soccer career he became a successful coach. He partook in shaping the philosophy and strategy that has defined Barcelona's team for the past three decades.

Short passing, flexibility, and fluid adaptability are reminiscent of Dutch tactics and Total Soccer. The only stain on Cruyff's close-to-immaculate career was the Netherlands' loss during the 1974 World Cup final against Beckenbauer's indefatigable German national team.

MAJOR HONORS
WORLD CUP RUNNER-UP: 1974
EREDIVISIE CHAMPION: NINE TIMES
KNVB CUP CHAMPION: SIX TIMES
LA LIGA CHAMPION: ONCE
COPA DEL REY CHAMPION: ONCE
EUROPEAN CUP: 1971, 1972, 1973
BALLON D'OR: 1971, 1973, 1974

CRUYFF

Cruyff was still at the top of his game during the 1978 World Cup, held in Argentina. However, he refused to participate in the tournament in protest against the Argentine military dictatorship. The Netherlands lost the final to Argentina. It is impossible to say, of course, but many believe that the Dutch team would have come out victorious if Cruyff had played.

The 1955–1956 season saw the launch of the European Cup tournament, which was later replaced by the UEFA Champions League. Stade de Reims (France) and Real Madrid (Spain) faced each other in the final. The French team was leading 2–0 but suddenly the Argentine forward Di Stéfano turned the tables and scored an elegant goal for Real Madrid, and the game finally ended with the Spanish team's victory. And so began the triumphant march of Real Madrid—and Di Stéfano. He was 30 years old but for five years led Real Madrid to victory in the European Cup. He scored one or more goals in all five finals and in the last one—a legendary 7–3 victory over Eintracht Frankfurt—the Argentine genius accomplished a hat trick. Di Stéfano was simply one of history's greatest soccer players—a powerful forward whose strength was no less in building up offensive play, and even defending against the opponents' offense. The ones lucky enough to observe Di Stéfano in action claim that only the upper echelon of the best can be considered his peers.

ARGENTINA FORWARD

INTERNATIONAL GAMES

COUNTRY	SEASON	TOTAL	GOALS
ARGENTINA	1947	6	6
COLOMBIA	1949–1952	7	6
SPAIN	1957–1961	31	23

MAJOR HONORS
COPA AMÉRICA CHAMPION: 1947
ARGENTINIAN CHAMPION: TWICE
COLOMBIAN CHAMPION: THRICE
LA LIGA CHAMPION: EIGHT TIMES
COPA DEL REY CHAMPION: ONCE
EUROPEAN CUP: 1956, 1957, 1958, 1959, 1960
BALLON D'OR: 1957, 1959

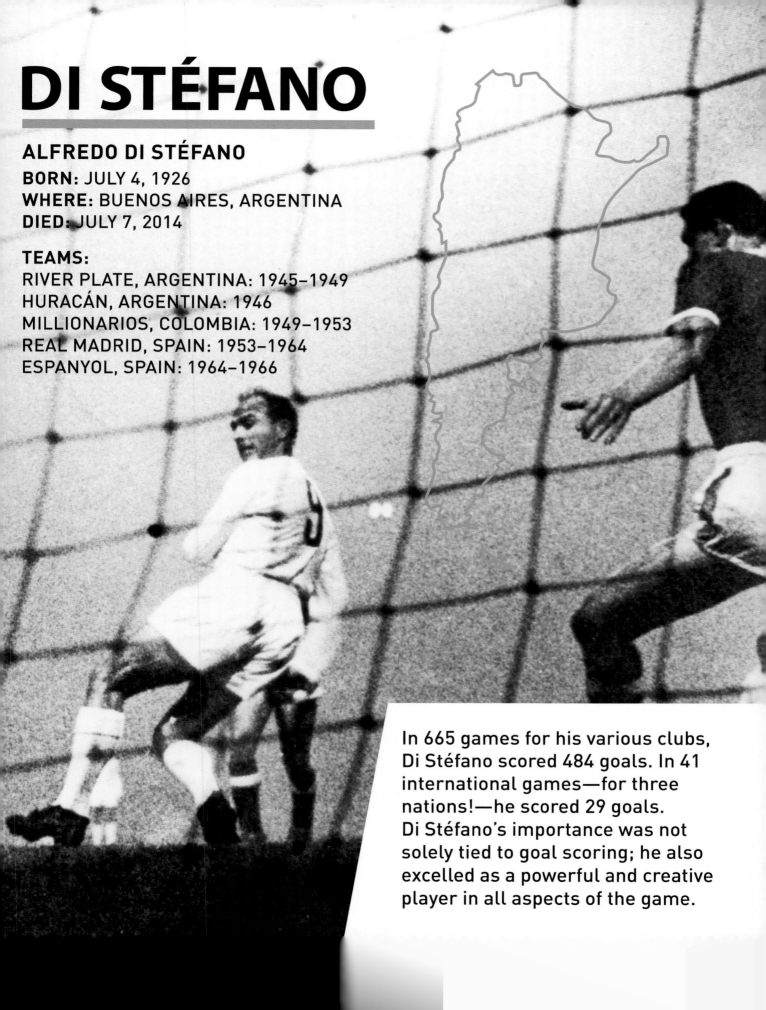

DI STÉFANO

ALFREDO DI STÉFANO

BORN: JULY 4, 1926
WHERE: BUENOS AIRES, ARGENTINA
DIED: JULY 7, 2014

TEAMS:
RIVER PLATE, ARGENTINA: 1945–1949
HURACÁN, ARGENTINA: 1946
MILLIONARIOS, COLOMBIA: 1949–1953
REAL MADRID, SPAIN: 1953–1964
ESPANYOL, SPAIN: 1964–1966

In 665 games for his various clubs, Di Stéfano scored 484 goals. In 41 international games—for three nations!—he scored 29 goals. Di Stéfano's importance was not solely tied to goal scoring; he also excelled as a powerful and creative player in all aspects of the game.

EUSÉBIO

FULL NAME: EUSÉBIO DA SILVA FERREIRA
BORN: JANUARY 25, 1942
WHERE: LOURENCO MARQUES, MOZAMBIQUE
DIED: JANUARY 5, 2014
HEIGHT: 5FT 9IN

TEAM:
BENFICA, PORTUGAL: 1960–1975

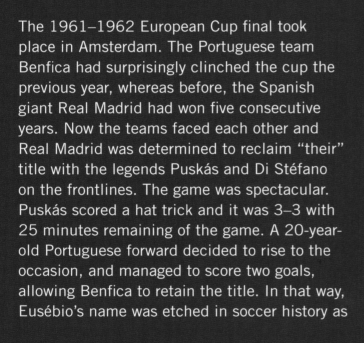

The 1961–1962 European Cup final took place in Amsterdam. The Portuguese team Benfica had surprisingly clinched the cup the previous year, whereas before, the Spanish giant Real Madrid had won five consecutive years. Now the teams faced each other and Real Madrid was determined to reclaim "their" title with the legends Puskás and Di Stéfano on the frontlines. The game was spectacular. Puskás scored a hat trick and it was 3–3 with 25 minutes remaining of the game. A 20-year-old Portuguese forward decided to rise to the occasion, and managed to score two goals, allowing Benfica to retain the title. In that way, Eusébio's name was etched in soccer history as one of the world's most incredible forwards.

He is inarguably Africa's best soccer player, having been born in Mozambique, which was then a Portuguese colony. His father was from Portugal, his mother from Mozambique. Eusébio led Portugal to their third World Cup victory in 1966, the country's biggest achievement. He was the top goal scorer, with nine goals in six games. Eusébio was an eager goal scorer and a powerful forward, whose style was defined by elegance and grace. He was nicknamed the "Black Pearl," and deservedly so. Spanning his 15-year career, he played 440 games with Benfica and scored 473 goals—more than one goal per game!

Eusébio was raised in conditions of abject poverty in Mozambique. When he was a boy, he played soccer with his friends, barefoot in the streets because none of them could afford proper soccer shoes. Neither did they own a soccer ball, so they played instead with a stuffed sock. However, the swift goal scorer had one thing in abundance: talent! And the legendary Di Stéfano claimed that Eusébio was the greatest soccer player he had ever witnessed.

PORTUGAL
(MOZAMBIQUE)
FORWARD

MAJOR HONORS
PORTUGUESE CHAMPION: ELEVEN TIMES
PORTUGUESE CUP CHAMPION: FIVE TIMES
EUROPEAN CUP CHAMPION: 1962
BALLON D'OR: 1965

GARRINCHA

BRAZIL
FORWARD

GARRINCHA

FULL NAME: MANUEL FRANCISCO DOS SANTOS
BORN: OCTOBER 18, 1933
WHERE: PAU GRANDE, BRAZIL
DIED: JANUARY 20, 1983
HEIGHT: 5FT 6½IN

TEAM:
BOTAFOGO, BRAZIL: 1953–1965

INTERNATIONAL GAMES: 1955–1966
TOTAL: 50
GOALS: 17

MAJOR HONORS
WORLD CUP CHAMPION: 1958, 1962
BRAZILIAN CHAMPION: TWICE

Soccer legend Pelé suffered an injury at the beginning of the 1962 World Cup, and as a result it was uncertain whether Brazil could defend the World Cup title. At this stage, the winger Garrincha entered the scene, inspiring the team with his incredible dexterity, and ball control that bordered on being otherworldly. He had been a member of the 1958 World Cup team, but this time around he truly exhibited his magical skills. "What planet is Garrincha from?" awe-struck journalists asked when he sped past one opponent after the other, making elegant assists or scoring goals himself.

He gave a multifaceted performance in the final despite a high fever, was elected best player of the tournament, and was joint-top goal scorer, with four goals. Garrincha's ball control was precisely that aspect of soccer in which Brazilians believed they had the strongest lead. He was an artist who mirrored Brazilian consciousness, no less than Pelé. Garrincha's success is even more impressive considering the fact that he struggled with a physical disability; his left foot was a couple of inches shorter than his right leg.

Manuel dos Santos was so small and birdlike in his movements and nimbleness that his sister began calling him "Little Bird"—"Garrincha." The name stuck. Outside of the field, Garrincha's life was difficult. He suffered from alcoholism, and after his soccer career was over, he lost all control and died tragically young at only 49.

DIEGO MARADONA

BORN: OCTOBER 30, 1960
WHERE: BUENOS AIRES, ARGENTINA

TEAMS:
BOCA JUNIORS, ARGENTINA: 1981–1982
BARCELONA, SPAIN: 1982–1984
NAPOLI, ITALY: 1984–1991
SEVILLA, SPAIN: 1992–1993

INTERNATIONAL GAMES: 1977–1994
TOTAL: 91
GOALS: 34

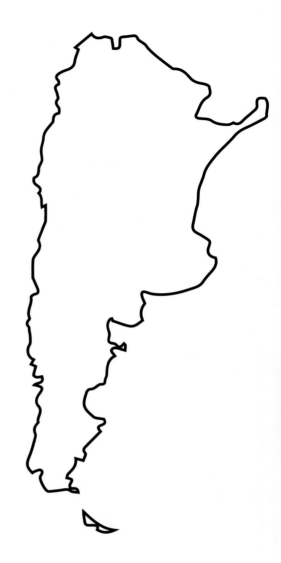

Maradona is the genius incarnate who conquers the world in one arena but falters in another. The Argentine player was the world's greatest in the nineties, and when he was at his best he equaled Pelé—and some believe that Maradona was even superior to the Brazilian. In the summer of 1986 Maradona made an individual achievement that is unprecedented in soccer history. The Argentine national team that participated in the World Cup in Mexico was filled with average players in comparison to the teams of West Germany, France, and Brazil, who were all full of highly skilled players—except in one way. Maradona played for Argentina and almost single-handedly pulled his team to the final, where it won a 3–2 victory over the combative Germans in a famous game.

Maradona had a tendency of getting into conflict with others, and his drug addiction had a severe and negative effect on his performance. The end of his career was tragic; he had successfully coached the national team for a time, but he was eventually made redundant. This inconsistent soccer player will nevertheless be cherished and adored for his achievements on the soccer field, and he is still worshiped almost like a god in Argentina.

MAJOR HONORS
WORLD CUP CHAMPION: 1986
WORLD CUP RUNNER-UP: 1990
COPA DEL REY CHAMPION: 1983
SERIE A CHAMPION: TWICE
COPPA ITALIA: 1987
UEFA CUP: 1989

ARGENTINA
FORWARD

MARADONA

Maradona exhibited both sides of his turbulent character during Argentina's 2–1 victory against England in the 1986 World Cup. First, he scored a goal by intentionally using his hand (now known as the "Hand of God" goal). Then he scored another goal, considered one of the World Cup's finest, by dashing across the field, dribbling past the entire England defense, and then steadily gliding the ball into the goal.

LIONEL MESSI

BORN: JUNE 24, 1987
WHERE: ROSARIO, ARGENTINA
HEIGHT: 5FT 7IN

TEAM: BARCELONA, SPAIN, FROM 2004–

INTERNATIONAL GAMES: FROM 2005–
TOTAL: 140
GOALS: 71

Anyone who watched Lionel Messi play soccer as a young boy saw that he had immense potential in the sport, despite his reserved character. Messi would outrun and easily dodge past much older boys. However, there was a danger that Messi would never be able to fully realize his talents. He suffered from a growth-hormone deficiency, which meant that his height would possibly not reach above five feet. At that height he would be unable to make it to the very top, regardless of his agility. Neither his parents nor the Argentine teams could afford to pay for the daily hormone injections that Messi required. Events took an unexpected turn when the Barcelona powerhouse came to the rescue. Representatives from the Spanish team had observed the talents of the 13-year-old Messi, and he was immediately called upon to join Barcelona. The club paid for the hormone injections, and soon Messi began to grow taller. Given Messi's incredible talent, it is safe to say that the team has long since received a return on the investment!

MESSI

Messi is the holder of so many goal-scoring records and garnered so many awards that it is virtually impossible to count them all. In 2012, Messi made another record that will not easily be broken when he scored a total of 91 goals in one year for club and country (Barcelona and Argentina). This is equivalent to a goal every fourth day over the whole year.

ARGENTINA
FORWARD

Messi is a true artist with the soccer ball. He is one of the most agile players to have ever entertained audiences of the sport and in nearly every game he offers a magical performance that few players can even come close to. At his best he is an unstoppable goal-scoring machine, but it is his tricks and cunning on the field that truly showcase his genius. And he has many years to come to show off his skills!

MAJOR HONORS
FIFA WORLD CUP RUNNER-UP: 2014
COPA AMÉRICA RUNNER-UP: 2007, 2015, 2016
LA LIGA CHAMPION: TEN TIMES
COPA DEL REY CHAMPION: SIX TIMES
UEFA CHAMPIONS LEAGUE: 2005, 2009, 2011, 2015
FIFA CLUB WORLD CUP: THREE TIMES
BALLON D'OR: 2009, 2010, 2011, 2012, 2015, 2019

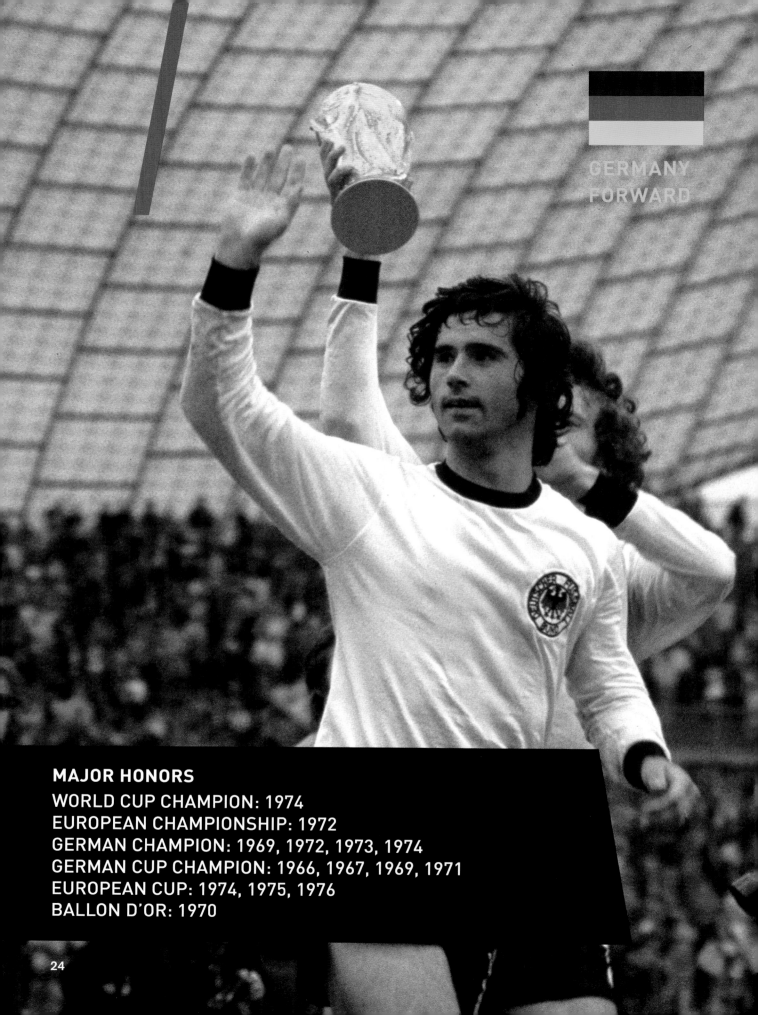

MAJOR HONORS

WORLD CUP CHAMPION: 1974
EUROPEAN CHAMPIONSHIP: 1972
GERMAN CHAMPION: 1969, 1972, 1973, 1974
GERMAN CUP CHAMPION: 1966, 1967, 1969, 1971
EUROPEAN CUP: 1974, 1975, 1976
BALLON D'OR: 1970

MÜLLER

GERD MÜLLER
BORN: NOVEMBER 3, 1945
WHERE: NÖRDLINGEN, GERMANY
HEIGHT: 6FT 1IN

TEAMS:
NÖRDLINGEN, GERMANY: 1963–1964
BAYERN MÜNCHEN, GERMANY: 1964–1979
FORT LAUDERDALE, USA: 1979–1981

Following the 1974 World Cup in West Germany, Müller declared his retirement from the national team. He was then only 28 years old. He therefore "only" managed to play 62 international games, scoring an amazing total of 68 goals!

For unknown reasons, soccer commentators are sometimes in disagreement on whether to include Gerd Müller on the list of the greatest soccer players in history. He was perhaps not the most charming player, and a vast bulk of his goals he scored by being at the right place at the right time, as the ball rolled inside the penalty box. Yet his vision was close to impeccable. He was a penalty-box predator of the highest caliber, and was absolutely unparalleled in that regard. His shots came with such force that he was nicknamed "Der Bomber," which referred to the unstoppable explosive power in his muscled thighs.

Müller cared little for running and was rarely seen dashing across the field, but if he chanced upon the ball at the right moment, he could accelerate with such speed that it would leave his opponents spinning. And though he could come across as immobile, he could turn around on the spot and he would always head in one direction: toward the opponents' goal. He easily counts among the greatest goal-racking machines in history. And despite claims to the contrary, he was always acutely aware of his position and variations in speed, which allowed him to burst ahead over short distances.

PELÉ

**BRAZIL
FORWARD**

MAJOR HONORS
FIFA WORLD CUP: 1958, 1961, 1970
BRAZILIAN CHAMPION: SIX TIMES
COPA LIBERATADORES: 1962, 1963

PELÉ
FULL NAME: EDSON ARANTES DO NASCIMENTO
BORN: OCTOBER 23, 1940
WHERE: TRÊS CORAÇÕES, BRAZIL
HEIGHT: 5FT 8IN

TEAMS: SANTOS, BRAZIL, 1956–1974
NEW YORK COSMOS, USA, 1974–1977

INTERNATIONAL GAMES: 1958–1971
TOTAL: 91
GOALS: 77

By 1958, Brazil had been considered one of the world's strongest soccer nations for decades, even though the national team had never managed to bring home the World Cup title. The 1950 Brazilian team comprised nothing but soccer geniuses, yet the team lost in the World Cup final on their home field, much to the dismay of the Brazilian nation. Eight years later, the World Cup was hosted by Sweden. The Brazilians had a strong team, though it was unclear whether the team would stand a chance against Europe's most powerful teams. As it turned out, a 17-year-old became the deciding player. One of the world's greatest soccer stars had now entered the scene: Pelé. He played as an attacking midfielder and was unparalleled in racking up goals.

During the 1958 FIFA World Cup final, Pelé scored two goals in a 5–2 victory over Sweden, thereby becoming a national hero in Brazil, which could finally celebrate its long-awaited World Cup victory. Pelé was in top form at the 1970 FIFA World Cup, and showed his true versatility on one of the greatest soccer teams in history.

Few players had Pelé's agility, which, coupled with his power, cunning, and restraint, made him a truly versatile player. When he was in his prime, Pelé's incredible moves on the field left the audience in awe. Pelé was a true winner, and he is found on top of most lists that enumerate the world's greatest soccer players.

According to official numbers, Pelé scored a total of 1,283 goals in 1,363 games over his career. He scored a whopping total of 92 hat tricks. In 1961, the president of Brazil declared him a "national treasure," which meant that Pelé could not be "sold" out of the country. Pelé was therefore never contracted with major European teams. However, he traveled to the US at the end of his career, where he played for the New York Cosmos.

MAJOR HONORS
EUROPEAN CHAMPIONSHIP: 1984
FRENCH CHAMPION: 1981
COUPE DE FRANCE: 1978
ITALIAN CHAMPION: 1984, 1986
COPPA ITALIA: 1983
EUROPEAN CUP: 1985
BALLON D'OR: 1983, 1984, 1985

PLATINI

MICHEL PLATINI
BORN: JUNE 21, 1955
WHERE: JOEUF, FRANCE
HEIGHT: 5FT 10IN

TEAMS:
NANCY, FRANCE: 1972–1979
SAINT-ETIENNE, FRANCE: 1979–1982
JUVENTUS, ITALY: 1982–1989

INTERNATIONAL GAMES: 1976–1987
TOTAL: 72
GOALS: 41

The 1984 European Championship tournament was the most glorious event in Michel Platini's soccer career. France played on home field and boasted a powerful team, but it was Platini who was the decisive factor. In fact, Platini was not a natural-born goal scorer, but he came into his own during the Euro tournament. He scored in every game that France played in the group stages, six goals in three games. During the semifinals, Platini scored France's winning goal in the 119th minute in extra time against Portugal.

He then flourished in the final against Spain, scoring the first goal in a 2–0 match. Thus he scored eight goals in six games, despite opponents' efforts to keep him in check. Platini was by nature a number "10," that is, the one who directs the flow of the offense. He was not exactly strapping and sometimes he even seemed lethargic, but his precision passes, majestic ball control, vision, and understanding of the game all made him an exceptional soccer player. Platini excelled in free kicks and scored numerous beautiful goals in these dead-ball situations. First and foremost, he was an intelligent player, and as Pelé said about him, "He used his head." Sadly, Platini's reign as president of the UEFA ended in disgrace, when he was found guilty of improperly pocketing £1.3 million given to him by Sepp Blatter.

Platini is the first player, after Johan Cruyff, to win three Ballon d'Or awards as Europe's greatest soccer player. He was the first to receive the award three consecutive years—the result of his fantastic performance as a playmaker with Juventus along with his 1984 World Cup title. The only players to receive three Ballon d'Or awards are Van Basten, Messi, and Cristiano Ronaldo. Of those, Messi is the only one to win three consecutive Ballon d'Or awards like Platini (and Messi has in fact won four consecutively).

FERENC PUSKÁS

BORN: APRIL 1, 1927
WHERE: BUDAPEST, HUNGARY
DIED: NOVEMBER 17, 2006
HEIGHT: 5FT 7½IN

TEAMS:
HONVÉD, HUNGARY: 1943–1955
REAL MADRID, SPAIN: 1958–1966

INTERNATIONAL GAMES FOR HUNGARY: 1945–1956
TOTAL: 85
GOALS: 84
INTERNATIONAL GAMES FOR SPAIN: 4

With much of Europe in ruins following the Second World War, Hungary's national soccer team emerged. It ranks among the greatest in history. The tightly knit and swift offensive team plowed down all rivals. The Hungarians were near invincible for years, and racked up one goal after the other. They did, however, experience a surprising defeat during the 1954 World Cup against West Germany. The team had several amazing goal scorers. Sándor Kocsis, for example, scored 75 goals in 68 international games. Yet Ferenc Puskás reigned supreme as the team captain.

He seemed able to simply will the ball into the net, but he also led the offense like a military commander. In fact, he was nicknamed the "Galloping Major." Puskás scored 352 goals in 341 games with his Hungarian team. After the Soviets invaded Hungary in 1956, the great Hungarian national team dissolved, and Puskás traveled to Spain, where he enjoyed a fruitful career with the historic Real Madrid team.

MAJOR HONORS
WORLD CUP RUNNER-UP: 1954
HUNGARIAN CHAMPION: FIVE TIMES
SPANISH CHAMPION: FIVE TIMES
COPA DEL REY CHAMPION: ONCE
EUROPEAN CUP: 1959, 1960, 1966

In 1971, Puskás served as coach of the Greek team Panathinaikos, and achieved the "impossible" by catapulting his team all the way to the European Cup final, which was a tournament that would later become the UEFA Champions League. The Greek team faced Ajax, led by captain Johan Cruyff, with coach Rinus Michels at the helm. These two men had developed the so-called Total Soccer concept, which had been inspired by the flowing tactics of the golden-age Hungarian team. Ajax won the game, and became European champions despite the heroic performance of Puskás's team.

RONALDINHO
FULL NAME: RONALDO DE ASSIS MOREIRA
BORN: MARCH 21, 1980
WHERE: PORTO ALEGRE, BRAZIL
HEIGHT: 5FT 11IN

TEAMS:
GREMIO, BRAZIL: 1998–2001
PARIS SAINT-GERMAIN, FRANCE: 2001–2003
BARCELONA, SPAIN: 2003–2008
AC MILAN, ITALY: 2008–2011
THEN A NUMBER OF TEAMS IN BRAZIL AND MEXICO

INTERNATIONAL GAMES: 1990–2013
TOTAL: 97
GOALS: 33

MAJOR HONORS
WORLD CUP CHAMPION: 2002
SPANISH CHAMPION: 2005, 2006
COPA LIBERTADORES: 2013 (WITH ATLÉTICO MINEIRO)
UEFA CHAMPIONS LEAGUE: 2006
BALLON D'OR: 2005

There is fierce competition between fans of the Spanish teams Real Madrid and Barcelona. On November 19, 2005, Barcelona visited Real Madrid's home field, Santiago Bernabeu. Both teams were crowded with outstanding players and the game was one for the history books. One man stood out in particular—Barcelona's left winger, Ronaldinho—who gave an absolutely riveting performance in the game. With incredible speed, technique, tricks, and joy, Ronaldinho dashed past one opponent after the other, leaving them in the dust.

He scored two great goals, both by racing from the halfway line and into Real Madrid's penalty box, and then firing a pointed shot past the goalkeeper Casillas. The cheerful wizard was a true all-rounder in Barcelona's 3–0 victory, and when he had scored the second goal, the awestruck Real Madrid fans honored him with a standing ovation. For Madrid fans to applaud a Barcelona goal is completely unheard of, and it shows how Ronaldinho spread contagious joy and garnered admiration for his pure talent, everywhere he went.

At the end of his twenties, the legendary Ronaldinho's enthusiastic and spirited nature began to wane, slowing down precisely at the point in his career where he should have been at his best. He would have most likely reached even higher levels, but his greatest moments will always be remembered.

RONALDINHO

CRISTIANO RONALDO

FULL NAME: CRISTIANO RONALDO DOS SANTOS AVEIRO
BORN: FEBRUARY 5, 1985
HEIGHT: 6FT 1IN

TEAMS:
SPORTING, PORTUGAL: 2002–2003
MANCHESTER UNITED, ENGLAND: 2003–2009
REAL MADRID, SPAIN: 2009–2016
JUVENTUS, ITALY: 2018–

INTERNATIONAL GAMES: FROM 2003–
TOTAL: 167
GOALS: 101

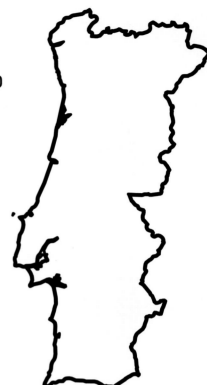

It is incredible how many soccer stars Portugal has produced over the years, given the size of the country, with a population of only 10 million. For example, Eusébio stars on page 16 of this book and the super-agile midfielder Luis Figo could easily have been included too—his brilliance won him the Ballon d'Or in 2000. Nevertheless, it is Ronaldo who reigns supreme!

In 2008, it seemed like Cristiano Ronaldo stood at the summit of the soccer world. He was a Champions League winner with Manchester United, and received the Ballon d'Or as Europe's greatest player. This vigorous goal scorer and lightning-quick winger was merely 23 years old, and anticipated a shower of recognition as the world's top star for many years to come. Then a young player from Argentina, Lionel Messi, entered the stage, who appeared even better than Ronaldo. And Messi won the Ballon d'Or for the following four years!

Ronaldo, however, was unfazed and as a true marker of his ambition, diligence, and vitality, pushed further in his training and scored even more goals. Through his hard work, he reaped another three Ballon d'Or awards, after a four-year hiatus. And then in 2017 he won the award for the fifth time. Cristiano Ronaldo is undoubtedly one of the greatest athletes of our times—he is powerful in diverse ways, though his mind is focused mainly on one thing: scoring goals! His goal-scoring records are innumerable, and he may well be capable of reaching even higher levels!

RONALDO

MAJOR HONORS
PREMIER LEAGUE: 2007, 2008, 2009
FA CUP CHAMPION: 2004
FOOTBALL LEAGUE CUP: 2006, 2009
LA LIGA CHAMPION: 2012, 2017
COPA DEL REY CHAMPION: 2011, 2014
UEFA CHAMPIONS LEAGUE: 2008, 2014, 2016, 2017, 2018
BALLON D'OR: 2008, 2013, 2014, 2016, 2017

RONALDO

RONALDO NAZÁRIO

FULL NAME: RONALDO LUÍS NAZÁRIO DE LIMA
BORN: SEPTEMBER 18, 1976
WHERE: RIO DE JANEIRO, BRAZIL
HEIGHT: 6FT

TEAMS:
CRUZEIRO, BRAZIL: 1993–1994
PSV, NETHERLANDS: 1994–1996
BARCELONA, SPAIN: 1996–1997
INTER MILAN, ITALY: 1997–2002
REAL MADRID, SPAIN: 2002–2007
CORINTHIANS, BRAZIL: 2008–2011

INTERNATIONAL GAMES: 1999–2013
TOTAL: 98
GOALS: 62

Ronaldo is often called "Il Fenomeno"— which means that he is like no other, a phenomenon. As a forward he is truly one of a kind, and in many ways, he was a trailblazer. Instead of waiting for the ball by the penalty box—which is usually the case with dangerous forwards—Ronaldo much preferred to receive the ball outside the box, and then fight his way to the goal with his incredible speed and determination.

At the same time, Ronaldo was agile like a cat, and could dribble the ball past the most hardened defenders. His goals were characterized by elegance and beauty, and there is no doubt that if he had not suffered from serious injury, this extraordinary genius would have achieved even more.

The night before the 1998 World Cup final, Ronaldo suffered a mysterious seizure, which led to a poor performance the following day in a game that Brazil lost. During the 2002 World Cup, on the other hand, Ronaldo was on top form, despite only having recently recovered from a two-year struggle with injuries. He scored both goals in a 2–0 victory over Germany in the final, and he scored a total of eight goals during the tournament. Many regret that Brazil's coach did not play him during the 1994 World Cup in the United States. He was then 17, bursting with talent and energy.

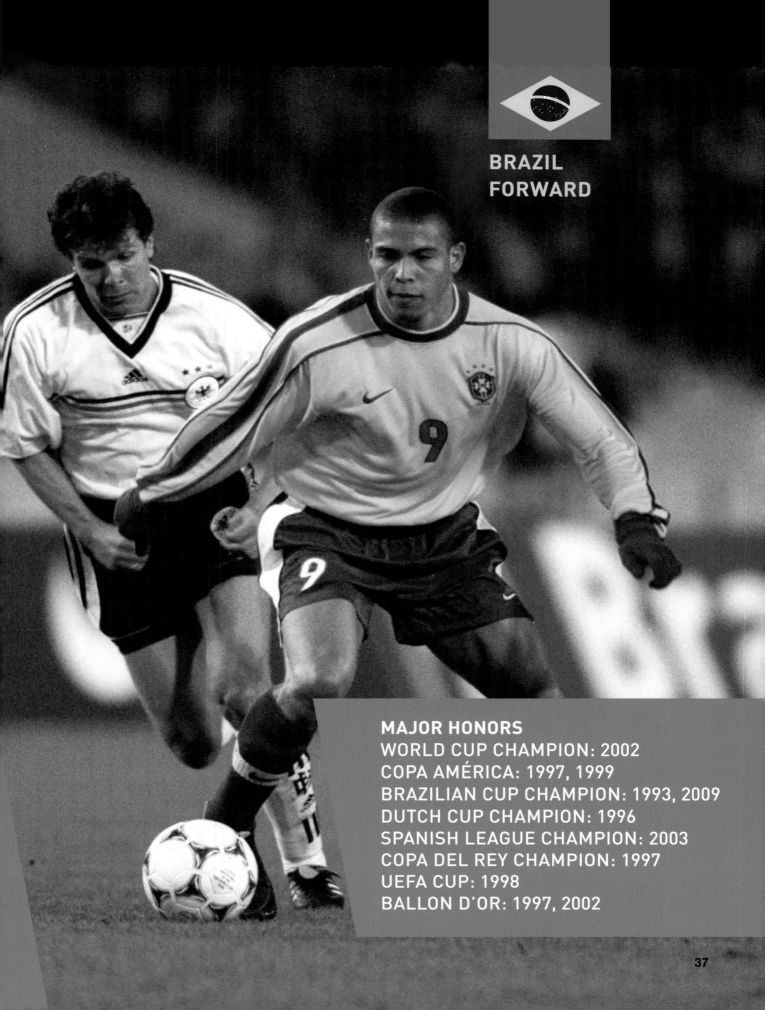

BRAZIL
FORWARD

MAJOR HONORS
WORLD CUP CHAMPION: 2002
COPA AMÉRICA: 1997, 1999
BRAZILIAN CUP CHAMPION: 1993, 2009
DUTCH CUP CHAMPION: 1996
SPANISH LEAGUE CHAMPION: 2003
COPA DEL REY CHAMPION: 1997
UEFA CUP: 1998
BALLON D'OR: 1997, 2002

VAN BASTEN

MARCO VAN BASTEN
BORN: OCTOBER 31, 1964
WHERE: UTRECHT, THE NETHERLANDS
HEIGHT: 6FT 2IN

TEAMS:
AJAX, NETHERLANDS: 1981–1987
AC MILAN, ITALY: 1987–1995

In the spring of 1993, a 28-year-old forward injured his ankle in a game with his team, AC Milan. An old injury had resurfaced with harrowing results; he would never play soccer again. He was one of most incredible forwards and impressive goal scorers of history, the Dutchman Marco van Basten. He had already accomplished remarkable achievements, first with Ajax and then with the historic AC Milan team, who some consider the most outstanding soccer team of all time. Van Basten had thrice received the Ballon d'Or. Only Cruyff and Platini had been bestowed with such an honor before him.

In 1988, he ensured UEFA Champions League victory for the Netherlands with one of the most beautiful goals ever seen in a major tournament final. Van Basten seized the ball in the air and assuredly fired a shot from the far corner, straight into the Soviet net. Van Basten was a fierce penalty-box predator but he also possessed great technique, keen vison, and charm. And he was supremely swift, despite his height and strong physique. Van Basten, and the Dutch nation, had great hopes that he would lead the country to victory at the 1994 World Cup, which would have marked the high point of his career, along with his companions Ruud Gullit, Frank Rijkaard, and others. Van Basten's 1993 injury perhaps did not change soccer history, but his achievements and classic talents will never be forgotten.

MAJOR HONORS
DUTCH CHAMPION: 1982, 1983, 1985
DUTCH CUP CHAMPION: 1983, 1986, 1987
ITALIAN CHAMPION: 1988, 1992, 1993, 1994
EUROPEAN CUP: 1989, 1990
UEFA EUROPEAN CHAMPIONSHIP: 1988
BALLON D'OR: 1988, 1989, 1992

Van Basten (right) with Ruud Gullit.

THE NETHERLANDS
FORWARD

The famous coach Fabio Capello, who led AC Milan for a time, claims that Van Basten is the most extraordinary forward that he has ever trained. When Diego Maradona was asked to name the greatest soccer player of history, he said: "It is either Romário or Van Basten." However, it must be said that Maradona made this remark before his fellow Argentine Messi had entered the spotlight.

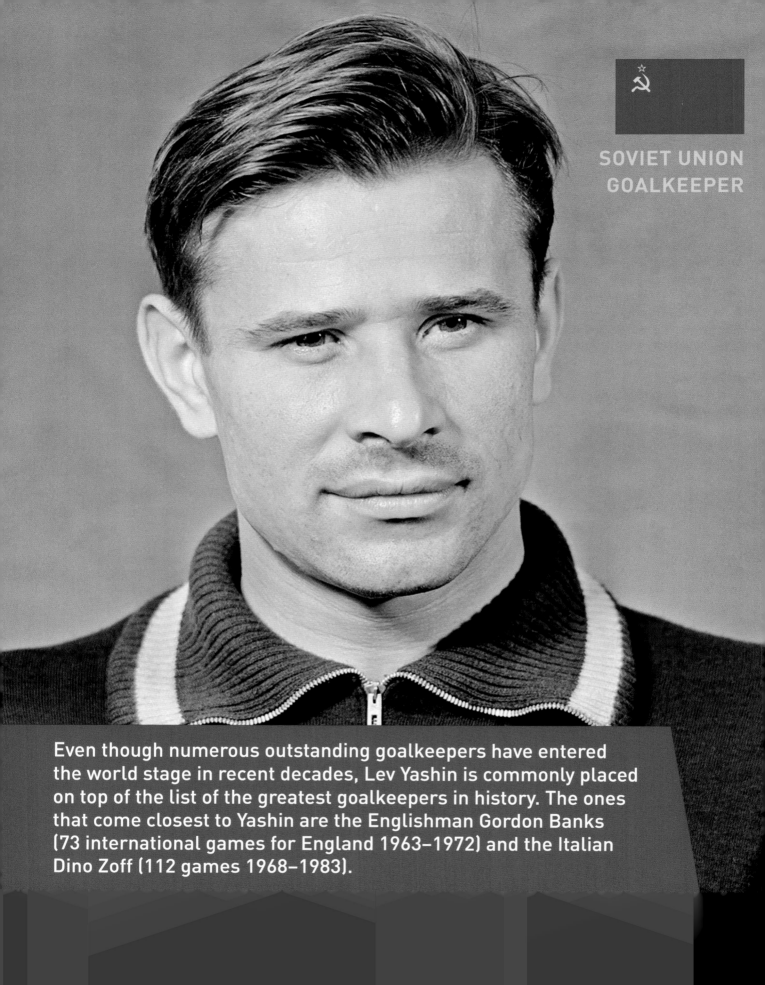

Even though numerous outstanding goalkeepers have entered the world stage in recent decades, Lev Yashin is commonly placed on top of the list of the greatest goalkeepers in history. The ones that come closest to Yashin are the Englishman Gordon Banks (73 international games for England 1963–1972) and the Italian Dino Zoff (112 games 1968–1983).

YASHIN

LEV YASHIN
BORN: OCTOBER 22, 1929
WHERE: MOSCOW, SOVIET UNION (RUSSIA)
DIED: MARCH 20, 1990 (ONLY 60 YEARS OLD)
HEIGHT: 6FT 2½IN

TEAM:
DYNAMO MOSCOW, RUSSIA: 1950–1970

The first UEFA European Championship tournament was held in 1960 in France. (The country would return as hosts in 2016.) Two soccer powerhouses—Yugoslavia and the Soviet Union (now both nonexistent)—met in the final. The game was even and went into extra time, and the winning goal was scored by the Soviets with little time left. The Soviet Union thereby became the first nation to win the European Championship. The remarkable goalkeeper Lev Yashin played a major part in the victory, and many consider him the greatest goalkeeper of all time. He was sometimes nicknamed the "Black Panther" due to his agility in the goal, but he was more commonly referred to as the "Black Spider." This moniker came from his tendency to wear a black uniform and because he seemed to have eight long and forceful arms that he would extend in every direction, to intercept even the most powerful shots. Some jested and claimed that he could change the course of the ball by simply peering at it. Yashin was in fact an innovative goalkeeper. Before his time, goalkeepers would normally stand rather motionless on the goal line, waiting for the ball to come their way.

Yashin's technique radically differed; he would command his defenders and maneuver beyond the goal line to hunt for the ball. His unprecedented performance during the 1958 World Cup deeply influenced goalkeepers around the world. Yashin is the only goalkeeper to receive the prestigious Ballon d'Or as Europe's greatest soccer player.

MAJOR HONORS
EUROPEAN CHAMPIONSHIP: 1960
EUROPEAN CHAMPIONSHIP
RUNNER-UP: 1964
SOVIET CHAMPION: FIVE TIMES
SOVIET CUP CHAMPION: THRICE
BALLON D'OR: 1963

ZICO

FULL NAME: ARTHUR ANTUNES COIMBRA
BORN: MARCH 3, 1953
WHERE: RIO DE JANEIRO, BRAZIL
HEIGHT: 5FT 7½IN

TEAMS:
FLAMENGO, BRAZIL: 1971–1983
UDINESE, ITALY: 1983–1985
FLAMENGO, BRAZIL: 1985–1989
KASHIMA ANTLERS, JAPAN: 1991–1994

INTERNATIONAL GAMES: 1976–1986
TOTAL: 71
GOALS: 48

World Cup results are not always fair and the best teams are not always triumphant. Most agree that the best team to NOT win the title was the Brazilian team during the 1982 World Cup. The team played beautiful and elegant soccer, which was like a foreboding of Cruyff's and later Guardiola's Barcelona at its best. And of all the geniuses on the team, one stood out: Zico. He was especially skilled with free kicks and playmaking, as well as having a keen eye for the opponents' goal.

Zico generally scored a goal in every other game, which is a ratio that any forward can be proud of. His free kicks were renowned, and he played so artfully that he became an embodiment of what Brazilians call "joga bonita" or "the beautiful game," which defines their preferred style of soccer. Even though Brazilians still mourn the fact that their team failed to bring home the World Cup title in 1982 and 1986, the conclusion of the 1978 World Cup was also tragic. With Zico at the helm, the team played well and lost none of the games it played, but due to peculiar organizational issues in the tournament, Brazil only managed to land third place.

MAJOR HONORS
BRAZILIAN CHAMPION: FOUR TIMES
COPA LIBERTADORES: 1981

ALTHOUGH BRAZILIANS GRIEVE THE WORLD CUP LOSSES SUFFERED BY THE GREAT NATIONAL TEAMS IN 1982 AND 1986, ZICO ALSO MISSED HIS CHANCE IN 1978.

BRAZIL
FORWARD

Zico played midfield in Brazil's 1982 World Cup team, along with legends such as Sócrates, Falcao, Toninho Cerezo, and Júnior. The World Cup tournament has probably never seen such a strong lineup of midfielders. The only thing that the team lacked was a world-class forward. All in all, Zico scored four goals in the tournament. The Brazilian team in the 1986 World Cup was composed of no fewer legends than before, but unfortunately, Zico was injured, and therefore unable to show his best.

ZIDANE

ZINEDINE ZIDANE
BORN: JUNE 23, 1972
WHERE: MARSEILLE, FRANCE
HEIGHT: 6FT 1IN
TEAMS:
CANNES, FRANCE: 1989–1992
BORDEAUX, FRANCE: 1992–1996
JUVENTUS, ITALY: 1996–2001
REAL MADRID, SPAIN: 2001–2006

INTERNATIONAL GAMES: 1994–2006
TOTAL: 104
GOALS: 31

Zidane's impressive soccer career came to a tragic end. The score was still 1–1 at the end of the 2006 World Cup final, in a face-off between France and Italy, and the game was moved into extra time. Zidane had scored France's goal from a penalty shot, and prepared himself to finish what he started and lead his team to victory. The Italian defender Materazzi then hurled some insulting words at Zidane, who lost his temper, and in a momentary rage, headbutted the Italian. Zidane was sent off as punishment, and France lost in the penalty shootout.

It is interesting to note that both representatives from France on the list of the world's greatest soccer players first proved their incredible skills with Juventus in Italy—first Platini and then Zidane. And they even played in a similar style. The strongest suit of both players was elegant ball control and technique, cunning, and vision. Both were playmakers, and played the position of attacking midfielder, scoring numerous goals. Zidane was however a slightly more dominant presence on the field than his older colleague, and his technique against the opponents' defense was noteworthy.

Zidane also managed to make France a world champion. It is generally agreed that without Zidane, France would have never clinched the World Cup title—which occurred on home field in France, in 1998, when Zidane scored two headers in a 3–0 victory over Brazil. His greatest goal, on the other hand, was for Real Madrid in a Champions League final. The Frenchman intercepted the ball in midair on the margins of the penalty box, and fired the ball directly into Bayer Leverkusen's goal.

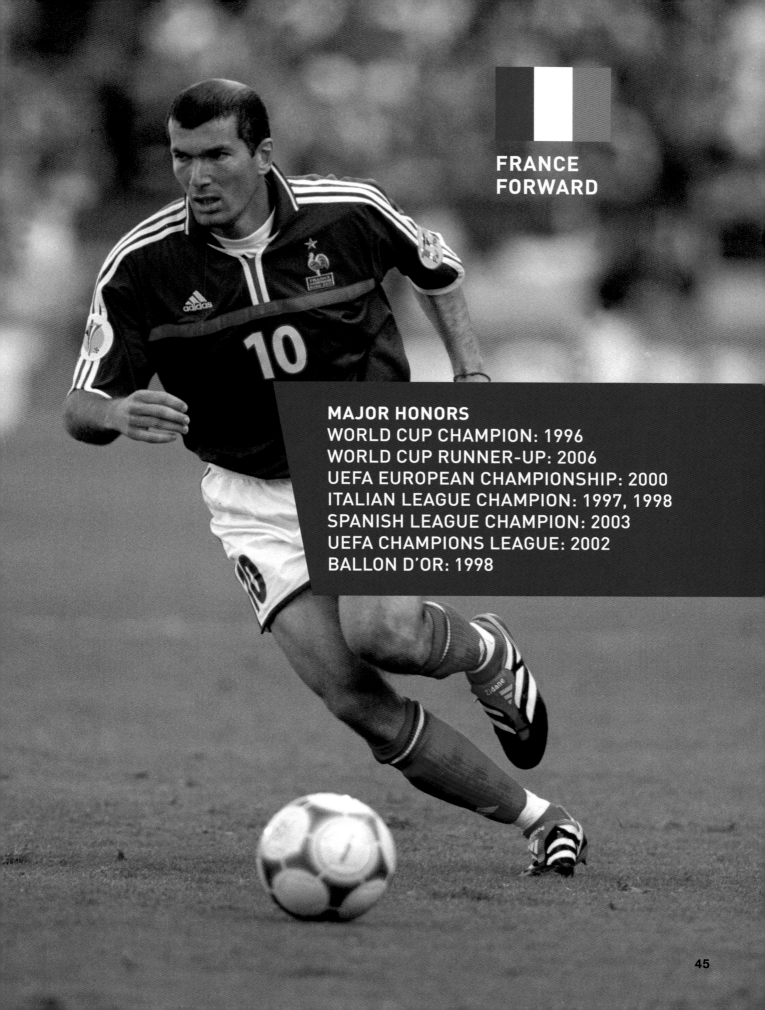

FRANCE
FORWARD

MAJOR HONORS
WORLD CUP CHAMPION: 1996
WORLD CUP RUNNER-UP: 2006
UEFA EUROPEAN CHAMPIONSHIP: 2000
ITALIAN LEAGUE CHAMPION: 1997, 1998
SPANISH LEAGUE CHAMPION: 2003
UEFA CHAMPIONS LEAGUE: 2002
BALLON D'OR: 1998

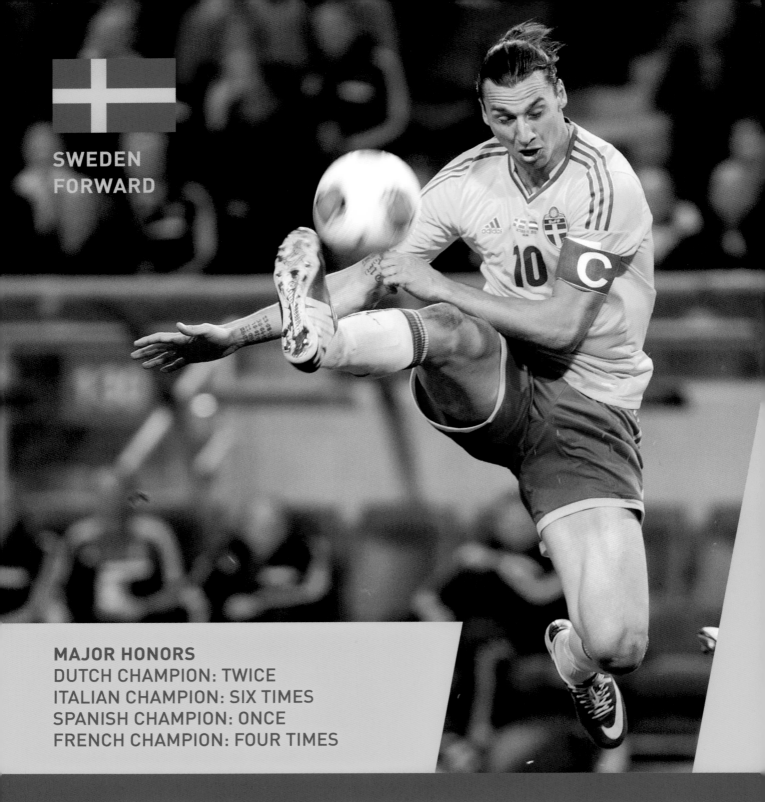

SWEDEN
FORWARD

MAJOR HONORS
DUTCH CHAMPION: TWICE
ITALIAN CHAMPION: SIX TIMES
SPANISH CHAMPION: ONCE
FRENCH CHAMPION: FOUR TIMES

ZLATAN

ZLATAN IBRAHIMOVIĆ
BORN: OCTOBER 3, 1981
WHERE: MALMÖ, SWEDEN
HEIGHT: 6FT 5IN

TEAMS:
MALMÖ, SWEDEN: 1996–2001
AJAX, THE NETHERLANDS: 2001–2004
JUVENTUS, ITALY: 2004–2006
INTERNAZIONALE, ITALY: 2006–2009
BARCELONA, SPAIN: 2009–2010
AC MILAN, ITALY: 2010–2012
PARIS SAINT-GERMAIN, FRANCE: 2012–2016
MANCHESTER UNITED, ENGLAND: 2016–2018
LA GALAXY, UNITED STATES: 2018–2020
AC MILAN, ITALY: 2020–

INTERNATIONAL GAMES: FROM 2001–
TOTAL: 116
GOALS: 62

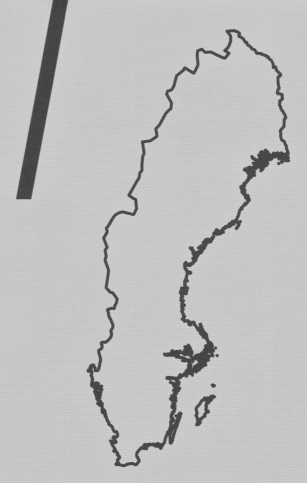

The Swedish genius Zlatan has made a host of records over his career, but his most unbelievable record is the following: From spring 2014, Zlatan won eight consecutive championship titles with five teams in three countries, all with top echelon teams. First, he clinched two championship titles, over a period of three years, with Ajax in the Netherlands, then two consecutive titles with Juventus in Italy, followed by three consecutive titles for Inter Milan in the same country, then yet another title with Barcelona in Spain during the 2009–2010 season. The following season Zlatan was champion once more with the Italian team AC Milan.

After this championship procession, Zlatan almost incredibly did not win anything for a whole year, but since then has managed to win an additional four titles with Paris St.-Germain. Given this flood of awards, it is safe to claim that Zlatan is a natural-born champion—as he in fact likes to claim himself. With his goal-scoring enthusiasm and magnetizing performances on the field, Zlatan is a fountain of joy, and there is always something exciting orbiting around him. Zlatan gets the ball rolling!

Zlatan is extremely nimble, despite his size, and he scores goals. One of his most famous goals was the fourth in Sweden's 4–2 victory over England in November 2012. Zlatan shot the ball with an overhead kick from a distance of almost 32 yards. "The most amazing goal I've ever seen!" shrieked the English commentator. And let's not forget that Zlatan was also responsible for the other three goals in the game.

MORE BESTS: BRAZIL

ROMÁRIO

Brazil has produced so many soccer legends over the years that it would take a mightily thick book to do them all justice. The troubled genius Romário de Souza Faria doubtlessly deserves to appear on the first pages of such a book. He was born in 1966, and with him on the frontlines, Brazil managed to clinch the long-desired world championship title in the USA in 1994, after almost a quarter-of-a-century wait. Romário sometimes appeared weary on the field, and other times his demeanor bordered on arrogance. Joining his team's defense was out of the question for him, and he generally liked to remain at the front of the field.

However, his body harbored incredible explosive power and skill, and he would only need a moment to shake off the defense and conjure mind-blowing goals. Injuries and lack of discipline prevented his career from flourishing further. He never made a name for himself with the European powerhouses, and he could have played more with the national team—but the moments when he collaborated with Ronaldo on the frontlines are truly unforgettable. As can be seen on p.39, Maradona held Romário in high esteem and another genius, Johan Cruyff, said of Romário that he was the greatest soccer player that he had ever trained. "He is completely unpredictable!" Cruyff exclaimed.

LEONIDAS

Leonidas da Silva (1913–2004) comes from the time around the first half of the twentieth century, when Brazil was rising as one of the most powerful soccer nations. He was a phenomenal forward, and many commentators claim that Leonidas invented the overhead kick, which he regularly demonstrated with spectacular results. He was the top goal-scorer at the 1938 World Cup, with seven goals in four games.

ZIZINHO

When Pelé entered the scene, he was generally considered to have created the role of the playmaking "number 10," the player who both scores goals and hunts goal-scoring opportunities for his teammates, as well as attracting rival defenders. However, Pelé said that he was influenced by Zizinho's (1921–2002) style, who served this role for the great Brazilian team in the 1950 World Cup. Born Thomaz Soares da Silva, Zizinho was highly skilled, an outstanding dribbler, excelled with headshots, had sharp vison, and could even play defense. According to Pelé, Zizinho "was the perfect soccer player."

RIVALDO

Born Rivaldo Vítor Borba Ferreira in 1972, this dynamic and skilled player is probably most famous for a spectacular overhead kick that he scored for Barcelona in a 2001 game against Valencia. He also played a critical role in the Brazilian national team that clinched the world championship title at the 2002 World Cup in Japan and South Korea. It is no coincidence that the road turned rocky for Brazil once Ronaldo, Ronaldinho, and Rivaldo left the national team.

BATISTUTA

The soccer fever in Argentina equals in pitch to that of their neighbors in Brazil, and the former has produced numerous great players. Argentine soccer is more often characterized by belligerence and fighting spirit than agility and dexterity, despite generating players such as Maradona and Messi. Outstanding forwards have regularly emerged in Argentina; the top goal scorer for the national team is still Gabriel Batistuta (b. 1969). He was a remarkable all-around goal scorer and the penalty box was his playground.

SANTAMARIA

While the legends Di Stéfano and Puskás racked up goals for Real Madrid during the first year of the European Cup, which the team won five consecutive years, the often-forgotten defense played no less of a part in that winning streak. The Uruguayan midfielder José Santamaria (b. 1929) stood sentinel for several years, and is considered by many to have been one of the world's best defenders.

ZANETTI

Javier Zanetti (b. 1973) enjoyed an unusually long soccer career, both with the Argentinian national team and his team Internazionale, where he played for 19 seasons. Zanetti retired in 2014, at the age of 41. From 1994–2011 he played in 143 international games. He intelligently read the game, and he could tirelessly dash the field in attacking play as well as deliver meticulous passes to his teammates.

MORE BESTS: SOUTH AMERICA

VARELA

The Uruguayan Obdulio Varela (1917–1996) was a decent soccer player, but those talents are not the reason he graces the pages of this book. As a matter of fact, he achieved one amazing and unique feat. In 1950, the Uruguayan national team played the last World Cup game against Brazil. They had to win in order to become world champions. However, the game took place on the Marcana field in front of a ferocious crowd of 200,000, who unanimously demanded victory for their team, and whose hatred for the Uruguayan team ran deep.

The Brazilian team was manned by powerful players in every post, with Zizinho in control. The Uruguayans played a strong defense during the first half, but the Brazilians slid in a goal in the beginning of the second half. Everyone expected that a shower of goals would now ensue. The relentless Varela then stirred his comrades to action with his fervent fighting spirit, shouting: "Now we win!" And in one of the most spectacular second halves in soccer history, the Uruguayans managed to score two goals and thereby snatch the World Cup title out of the Brazilians' hands.

MORE BESTS: ITALY

MEAZZA

This fantastic goal-scoring midfielder turned Italy into a superpower. Giuseppe Meazza (1910–1979) was captain and main goal scorer of the Italian national team that became world champions in 1934 and 1938.

MALDINI

Paolo Maldini was born in 1968, and played as a left back or central defender with AC Milan over his long career, from 1985 to 2009. He won seven Italian championship titles with the team as well as winning the Champions League five times! Many forwards, such as Ronaldo, Zlatan, and Ronaldinho, agree that Maldini was one of the greatest and most cunning defenders that they had ever played against. He was never rough, he had a comprehensive understanding of the game, and he could make passes that any great midfielder would be proud of.

RIVA & RIVERA

Luigi Riva (b. 1944) was one of Italy's most elegant goal scorers and even more so in the 1970 Italian national team. With the incredible power of his left foot, he shot the small team Cagliari into the big leagues, and in 1970 delivered them an Italian championship title. AC Milan player Gianni Rivera (b. 1943) was an attacking midfielder and goal-scoring machine, who flourished around the same time as Riva. Both these players played an important role in bringing fame to Italian soccer, which was defined by sophistication and elegance, though a sturdy defense was in actual fact the foundation. Later, Roberto Baggio would come to symbolize this style of soccer.

Riva Rivera

ZOFF

Gianluigi Buffon is nowadays Italy's most famous goalkeeper and he has long been considered one of the greatest goalkeepers in history. Italians though like to point out that Dino Zoff (b. 1942) was even better. Zoff concluded his outstanding career by becoming world champion in 1982, at 40 years old.

THE DEFENDERS

The Italians are renowned for their rigorously organized and even rough defense play. In this context, it is perhaps worth mentioning Gaetano Scirea (1953–1989), who was a pillar in the Italian team that unexpectedly won the 1982 World Cup title. Scirea died in a car accident at the age of 36. Franco Baresi (b. 1960), who was the backbone of the now historic AC Milan team, also deserves a mention. Fabio Cannavaro (b. 1973), who was known for his small build and exceptionally good manners—both unusual for an Italian defender!—was largely responsible for Italy's fourth world championship title in 2006.

MORE BESTS: EUROPE

GIGGS

This Welsh winger Ryan Giggs (b. 1973) was a lightning-quick and agile goal scorer, who in his best form was greatly reminiscent of George Best, and not solely because Giggs wore red throughout his career for Manchester United. Giggs's reputation was not only based on his bountiful talents, but also on his stamina and resilience. He played his first game for Manchester United in March 1991 and the last in May 2014. He was with the team for 24 seasons, and scored in all of them except for the last. He played 963 games and scored 163 goals—all top caliber games. He was English champion thirteen times, and was never once sent off for a foul in his whole time with Manchester United. And how the English dreamed of Giggs playing for their national team rather than the Welsh team!

MOORE & CHARLTON

England's only championship title at a major tournament arrived at the 1966 World Cup, on home field. With all due respect to other players, there were two in particular that stood out. The defense was led by the vigorous center back Bobby Moore (1941–1993), who played for West Ham for most of his soccer career. He was the first ever player to participate in more than 100 international games with England, and Pelé said that Moore was the most power-ful defender he had ever faced on the field.

Leading the midfield was another Bobby, the legendary Bobby Charlton (b. 1937). Charlton was a fierce attacker who was also cunning, with especially clear vision, and commanded his team in a way that was pure joy to observe. From 1956–1973, he played with Manchester United, and though many geniuses have joined the ranks of that particular team, Charlton has proven the most important one.

HENRY

France has produced a number of powerful forwards. At the 1958 World Cup in Sweden, Just Fontaine scored 13 goals in six games! However, the most talented of these forwards in recent memory is undoubtledly Thierry Henry (b. 1977) who began his career as a winger but later moved to the position of forward at the behest of Arsene Wenger when the former joined Arsenal in 1999. Over the next eight years, Henry racked up goals of every variety after which he transferred to Barcelona, where his soccer successes continued.

MÜLLER

Many believe that a new victorious dawn is rising for Germany, given the country's reign over the 2014 World Cup in Brazil. Germany possesses a great number of remarkable soccer players, and Thomas Müller (b. 1989) definitely counts among the best. He scored 10 goals during the World Cup before reaching the age of 25—and there is much more where that came from!

Xavi

Iniesta

XAVI & INIESTA

Spain became European champions in 1964, but struggled for a long time to reach the same heights at major tournaments. It was not until 2008 that Spain would see another championship title, finally delivered by the national team at the European Championship tournament held in Austria and Switzerland. And then began a shower of trophies. Spain won both the 2010 World Cup in South Africa and the 2012 European Championship hosted by Poland and Ukraine. No other team had accomplished such a feat before them.

The Spanish team was manned by exceptional players, yet no one doubted that this wave of victories was thanks to two players—the companions from Barcelona, Xavier Hernández (b. 1980) and Andrés Iniesta (b. 1984). Both mastered the short-passing technique adopted by Barcelona and the national team, and both players have excellent vision and oversight. Xavi's passes were near perfect, and it was impossible to steal the ball from Iniesta.

MORE BESTS: EUROPE

NEUER

Manuel Neuer (b. 1986) is a skilled and swift goalkeeper for Germany, and he has attracted attention for often playing way beyond the penalty box, where goalkeepers usually wait. Neuer likes to play almost as a "sweeper," distributing the ball from the back to his teammates. Neuer's tactics have now begun to spread around the world, as goalkeepers emulate his style.

MORE BESTS: AFRICA

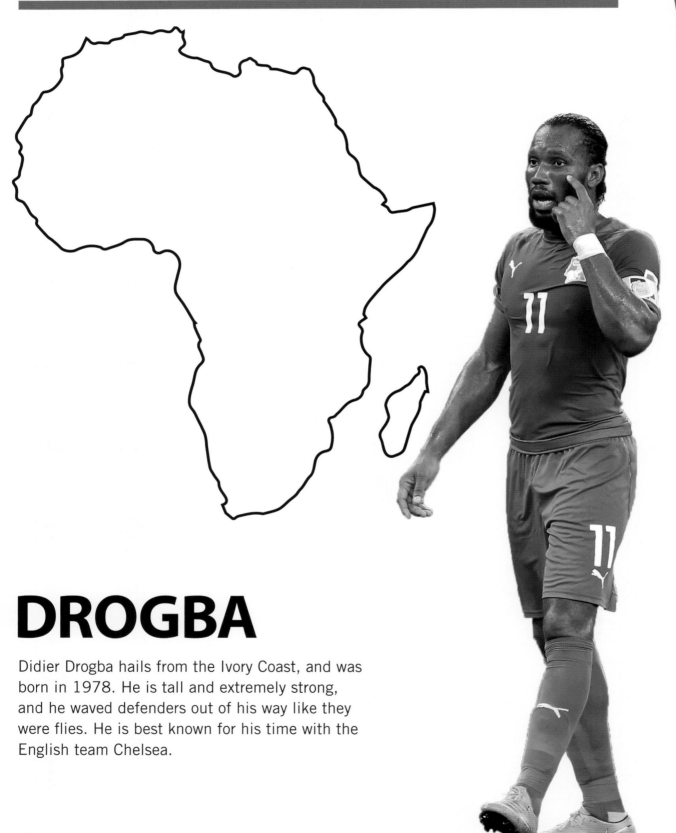

DROGBA

Didier Drogba hails from the Ivory Coast, and was born in 1978. He is tall and extremely strong, and he waved defenders out of his way like they were flies. He is best known for his time with the English team Chelsea.

WEAH

Eusébio probably remains the greatest African soccer player, but next in order is most likely the Liberian George Weah (b. 1966). He arrived in Europe in 1988, and played first with Monaco in France. At that time, it was a rare occurrence that an African soccer player would journey to Europe, but Weah became a huge success with his dazzling attacking play, and he racked up goals over the next years with one major team after the other.

He played with PSG, AC Milan, Chelsea, Manchester City, and Marseille. In 1995, he became the first ever African to win the Ballon d'Or. Weah was also intelligent and altruistic, and after he retired from soccer he became a respected politician and humanitarian in his home country.

ETO'O

Samuel Eto'o was born in Cameroon in 1981. He was an incredible goal scorer—fierce and agile at the same time. He was Spanish champion thrice with the remarkable Barcelona team, and scored 129 goals in 201 games. It speaks volumes that he was an inseparable part of a team that also boasted the legends Xavi, Iniesta, and Messi!

TOURÉ

Born in 1983, Yaya Touré, this big and vigorous midfielder from the Ivory Coast, has played an integral part in the powerful Manchester City team since 2010. Before, he played for three years with Barcelona. He has been named African player of the year four times.

DONOVAN

Landon Donovan was born in 1982 in California. This triumphant, energetic, and nimble forward has terrified many a goalkeeper. Donovan was a true legend, scoring 141 goals in 317 games over a period of 11 years with LA Galaxy, which translates to a goal in every other game.

These are incredible statistics, given that

Donovan often played as winger or attacking midfielder rather than an all-out striker. Donovan played in 157 international games for the US, and he holds the goal-scoring record, with a total of 57 goals. He was a passionate player, unpredictable, and had relentless fighting spirit—exactly the type of player that fans like to watch.

DEMPSEY

Clint Dempsey now threatens Donovan's goal-scoring record with the US national team, and he could break it at any moment! Dempsey, a Texan born in 1983, played for Fulham in the English Premier League and then for a time with Tottenham. He is a powerful and sharpshooting goal scorer and he has racked up goals for the Seattle Sounders—and the US national team.

MORE BESTS: USA

THE GOALKEEPERS

For some reason, most of the US players who have enjoyed the greatest success in Europe are goalkeepers.

Tim Howard (b. 1979) was born in New Jersey and transferred to Manchester United in 2003, where he became Premier League champion. He was then contracted with Everton in 2006, where he made a name for himself as one of England's greatest goalkeepers. As this is written, the dynamic Howard has guarded the goal in 121 games for the US national team.

Kasey Keller (b. 1969) also attracted attention with English teams such as Leicester and Tottenham, as well as with strong teams in Spain and Germany. Keller played in 102 international games.

Brad Friedel (b. 1971) played with Liverpool, Blackburn, Aston Villa, and Tottenham in England, and participated in 102 international games.

Tony Meola (b. 1969) played almost exclusively in the US, most prominently for the Kansas City Wizards, playing in a total of 100 international games.